The
Kew Gardens
Origami Flowers Book

Beautiful projects
inspired by nature

MONIKA CILMI

ARCTURUS

To my splendid mum, who has always believed in me.

Born in Italy and currently living in England, Monika Cilmi is
an artist, author and transformation life coach. Her passion for
Chinese and Japanese art is expressed through her work, which
includes calligraphy, painting, sculpture and crafts such as
origami, wrapping designs and paper dolls.

Photography: Will White

This edition published in 2020 by Arcturus Publishing Limited
26/27 Bickels Yard, 151–153 Bermondsey Street,
London SE1 3HA

Text and design copyright © Arcturus Holdings Limited
The Royal Botanic Gardens, Kew logo copyright © The Board of Trustees of the
Royal Botanic Gardens, Kew

ISBN: 978-1-83857-564-9
AD007508UK

Printed in China

Contents

Introduction

'Origami' is a Japanese portmanteau word that means 'folding paper'. An ancient art, origami still fascinates people today and in expert hands can produce splendid sculptures. Even the amateur origamist can make beautiful, imaginative shapes, sometimes with just a single piece of paper. I am always amazed by the new diagrams and designs I see, and they inspire me to create my own.

This book pays tribute to the world-famous Royal Botanic Gardens, Kew, in London, and reflects some of the beautiful plants in their collection. I hope it will stimulate your imagination and appreciation for the art of origami. It includes information about materials and folding techniques as well as a range of lovely projects. All it takes is a little determination and concentration, and you will master this delightful and surprising art.

Paper-folding – a history

Buddhist monks introduced paper to Japan in the late sixth century, and they used origami in ceremonies and rituals. The samurai also practised paper-folding. During the Edo period (1600–1868) and Genroku era (1688–1704), designers used images of origami cranes and boats on kimonos and clothing in general. The templates were passed on from generation to generation, both orally and by hand. The traditional type of Japanese origami paper is 'washi', which means 'handmade'. The characteristics of this paper (strong, pliable and textured) are essential for some types of origami. For example, the lotus pattern in this book will tear if made with ordinary rather than washi paper.

You will find that origami helps to improve various mental processes, including those of concentration, coordination and visualization. The act of reproducing previously created shapes is also great for dexterity and memory skills. To complete a model, the origamist must be able to picture it in three dimensions, which involves an understanding of geometric and spatial measurement.

Materials

Origami paper comes in various sizes and can be bought from specialist shops and online. In this book, I have used 15cm (6in) square paper, which I've cut into smaller sizes where necessary. There are many different types of origami paper, including:

- single-sided (one side coloured, the other side white)
- double-sided (different colours on each side)
- washi (textured, handmade paper ideal for intricate origami)
- chiyogami (paper patterned with traditional Japanese designs)
- shinwazome (thick, textured paper embossed with a raised pattern)
- unryu ('cloud dragon paper' – a beautiful textured paper with long fibres swirling through it)
- crêpe
- graduated colour

Try practising with single-sided paper so that you can see the folds and creases clearly. As other papers can be expensive, it's advisable to hone your skills

before experimenting with these. Origami flowers usually work well with crêpe paper because of its softness and texture. Some flowers, such as the hydrangea, look great made with graduated paper. I'd recommend using double-sided, patterned, crêpe, graduated and washi paper for the best results.

The other materials and tools used in this book include:

- pipe cleaners (for creating stems)
- florist's tape
- scissors
- tweezers
- glue (stick and craft)
- pencil

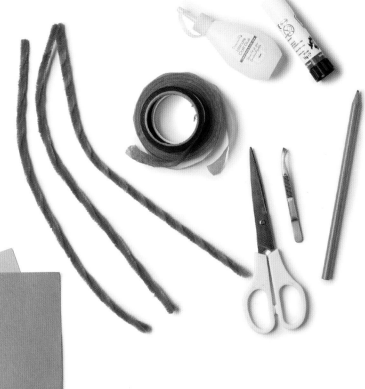

Folds

The two basic origami folds are the valley and the mountain, shown here.

 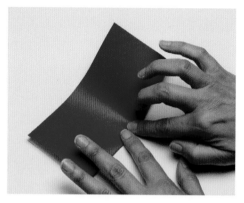

Fold the paper up edge to edge to make a valley fold.

Be sure to make a sharp crease so that the subsequent folds are crisp and accurate.

Fold the paper down edge to edge for a mountain fold.

This gives you the mountain shape.

A pleat fold is created by making a valley fold, followed by a mountain fold. A series of pleat folds creates a concertina effect.

Reverse folds
Inside and outside reverse folds take a bit of practice to get right.

Mountain-fold the paper, then fold the top corner, as shown. Fold in both directions, to make a good crease.

Open the folded corner and press in along the centre fold.

Flatten to create an inside reverse fold.

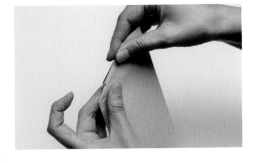

For an outside reverse fold, crease the corner as before, but this time fold the edge outwards, as shown.

Press inwards towards the 'v' shape you have created.

Press down and close the model.

Bases
Preliminary base

1 Fold the paper square in half both ways. Open it again.

2 Now fold on the diagonal both ways.

3 Keep it folded like this, with the long side at the bottom.

4 Reverse fold the right-hand side so that it is inside the shape.

5 Now reverse fold the left-hand side in the same way.

6 Your preliminary base should look like this.

Waterbomb base

1 Fold the paper in half once, then fold on the diagonal both ways. Open it again.

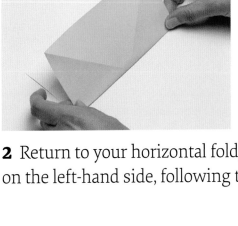

2 Return to your horizontal fold, and reverse fold the model in on the left-hand side, following the crease you have made.

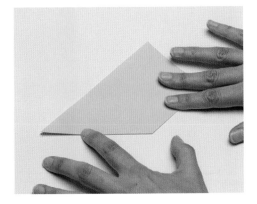

3 The shape will look like this.

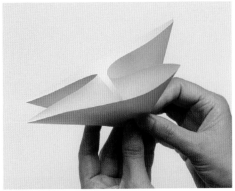

4 Now do the same on the right-hand side.

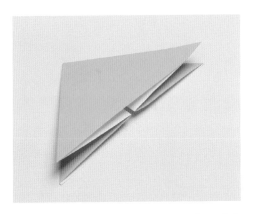

5 The waterbomb base should look like this.

1 Tulip

★★

The tulip is a type of lily. There are around 76 species of tulip. This model can be made in a range of colours or with graduated-tone paper.

FLOWER

1 Starting with a waterbomb base, fold the two top flaps towards the centre, as shown.

2 Turn the model over and repeat on the other side.

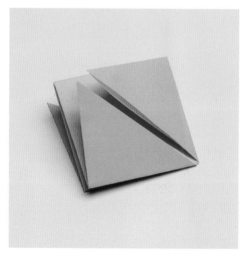

3 Fold the right-hand flap to the left and press down.

4 Fold the remaining flap on the right along the crease, as shown.

6 Turn the model over and repeat steps 3–5 on the other side.

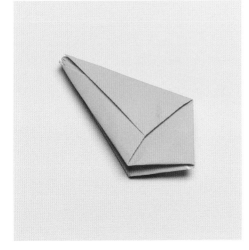

5 Tuck the left-hand flap into the pocket in the right-hand flap. Flatten the model.

7 Blow gently into the base of the model to inflate it.

8 Carefully open the external flaps to reveal the finished flower.

STEM AND LEAF

1 Fold the paper in half diagonally and reopen it.

2 Fold both edges to the centre.

3 Fold in the sides, as shown.

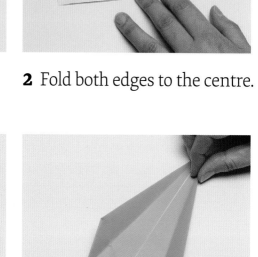

4 Fold in again, as shown. The model should look like the second photo, above.

5 Now crease and fold horizontally.

6 Valley fold the model along its length.

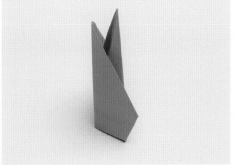

7 Stand the stem on its base and place the flower on top.

2 Hydrangea

★★

Hydrangeas are eye-catching, mop-headed plants often seen at the seaside. The flowers come in shades of white, pink, blue and green. You can use plain paper here, or a graduated-tone paper for a stunning effect.

FLORET

You need a small square for this, so cut your paper into four.

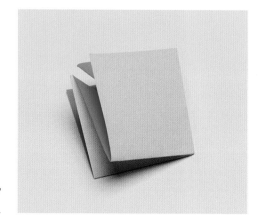

1 Using one of the four squares, make a preliminary base (colour inside).

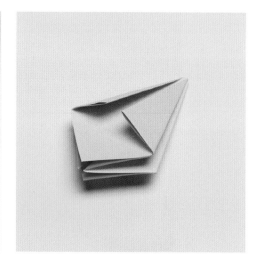

2 Fold in the sides of the top flap to the centre. (Note that the open edge of the base is bottom left in the photo.)

3 Turn the model over and repeat these steps on the reverse.

5 Unfold the model and open out the 'petals'.

4 Crease and fold horizontally.

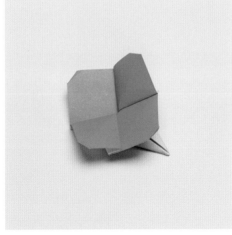

7 Make around 17 of these florets and glue them together to create the characteristic hydrangea mop-head.

6 Roll back the edges of the petals to create a curved shape.

LEAF

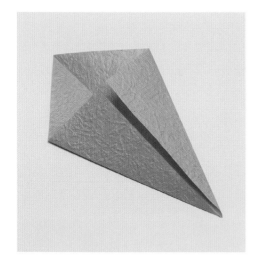

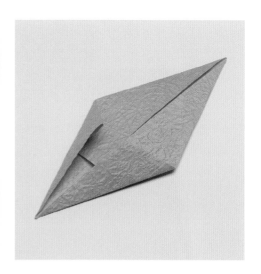

1 Using a sheet of textured paper 15cm (6in) square, repeat steps 1 and 2 of the tulip leaf (page 12).

2 Fold in both sides as shown.

3 Now crease the tip of the model and flatten down.

 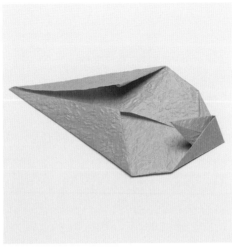

4 Fold the end of the tip in the opposite direction and flatten down, ensuring that it is in line with the centre of the model.

5 Valley fold the model in half lengthways.

6 Start folding in pleats from the bottom, as shown.

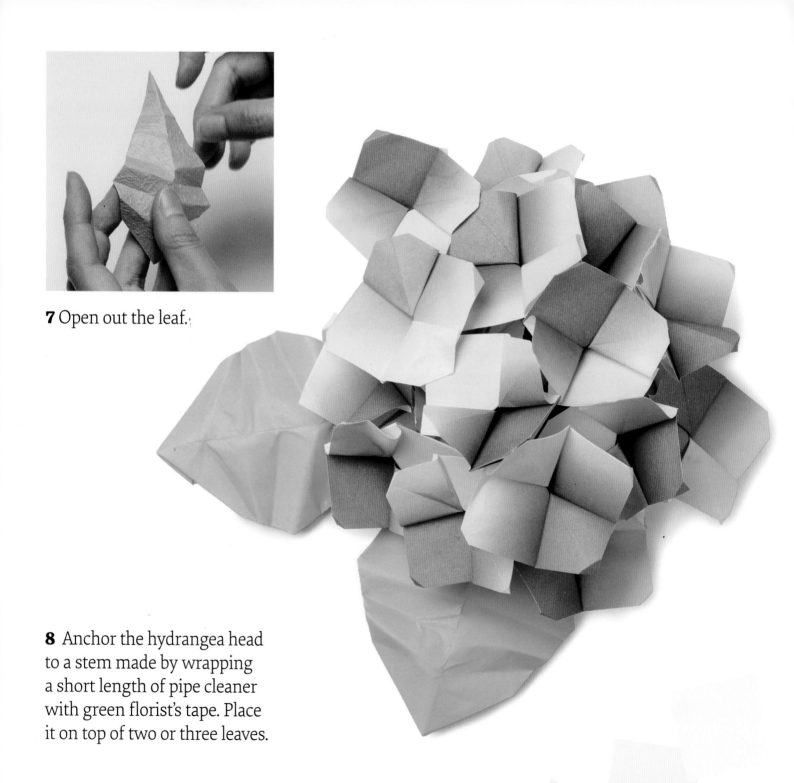

7 Open out the leaf.

8 Anchor the hydrangea head to a stem made by wrapping a short length of pipe cleaner with green florist's tape. Place it on top of two or three leaves.

FLOWER

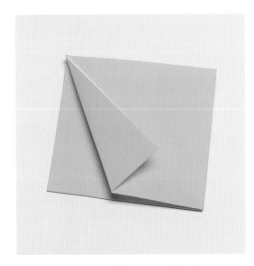

1 Starting with a preliminary base, fold one side towards the centre as shown.

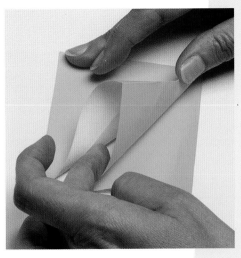

2 Rotate the model anticlockwise and open up the flap.

3 Rose

★★★

This fragrant rose is a rambling plant with single blooms. The model is best made with double-sided paper, but we have shown the steps using single-sided paper to make the folding process clear.

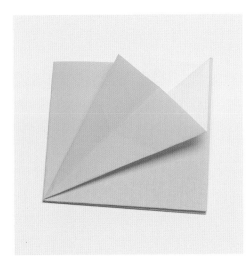

3 Rotate and flatten it down to give this kite shape.

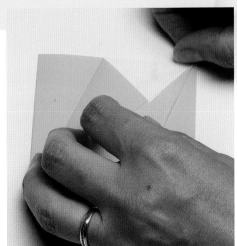

4 Fold the top edges of the kite to the centre and unfold again.

 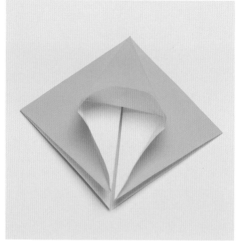

5 Rotate the model 180° and lift the flap as shown.

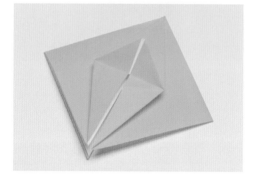

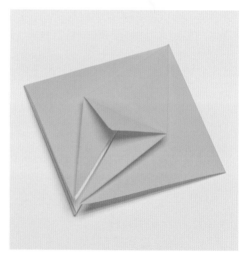 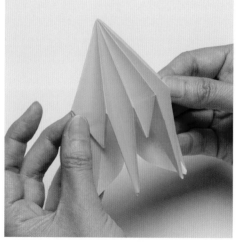 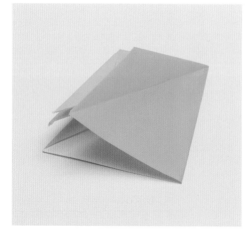

6 Fold the edges of the flap inwards, and press down.

7 Fold down the top flap.

8 Rotate the model to the starting point and repeat steps 1–7 on two further flaps, leaving the last one untouched.

9 Close the model.

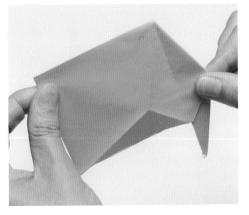  

10 Holding the model on both sides, open up the large flap and fold as shown to make a vertical crease.

11 Unfold and open the model.

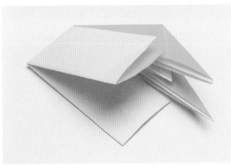

 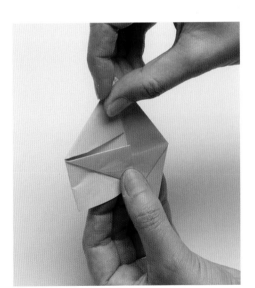

12 Fold back along the crease you have just made, and close the model again.

13 Fold both corners inwards so your model looks like this.

14 Open the lower flap and insert your finger underneath it, as shown.

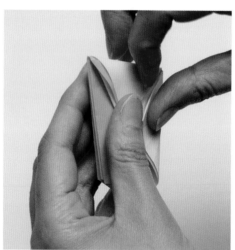

16 Turn the model over and fold in both corners on the other side.

17 Again, open the flap and flatten down.

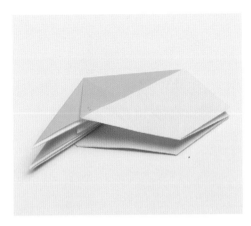

18 Your model should look like this.

19 Holding the model with the pointed flaps downwards, fold up the small triangles on both sides.

20 Fold up the pointed flaps. Inside reverse fold the top of the model.

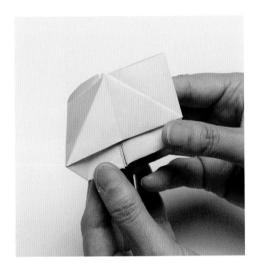

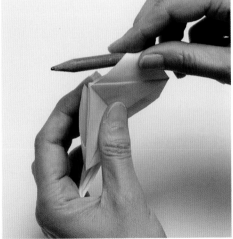

21 Rotate the model slightly and open the large flaps. Take a pencil and wrap each flap around it to give a 'curl'. The first petal is done. Make another four the same.

STAMENS

LEAF

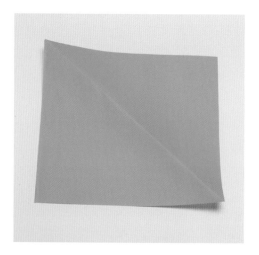

1 Take a sheet of paper measuring 7.5cm (3in) square and concertina fold it by making alternate mountain and valley folds.

2 Pinch in the middle and twist the bottom half to secure it. Make two more the same.

1 Take a sheet of paper measuring 15cm (6in) square and fold on the diagonal.

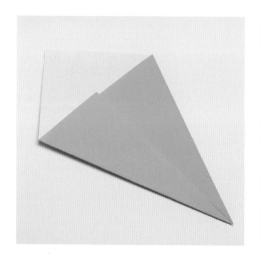

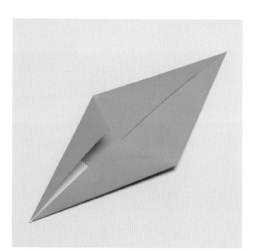

2 Fold in the sides to the centre to create a kite shape.

3 Fold in the corners to make a diamond shape.

4 Fold edge to edge on the diagonal, as shown.

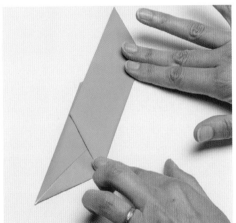

5 Fold in half on the diagonal again. Make a second leaf the same.

PUTTING IT ALL TOGETHER

Assemble the rose by glueing the petals together and pushing the stamens through the centre. Glue the leaves to the back of the model.

4 Lotus

★

The lotus is an aquatic plant which can be found in the Waterlily House at Kew. This exotic flower is sacred to Hindus and Buddhists. The delicate origami model shown here is best made with thin, double-sided washi paper as the successive folding will cause ordinary paper to tear.

1 Fold your sheet of paper in half and in half again. Open it out.

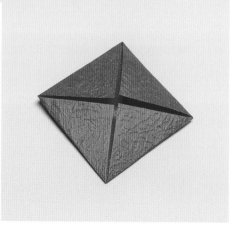

2 Fold all four corners to the centre.

3 Fold in all four corners again to make a smaller square.

4 Turn the model over and repeat the folding (it will become quite fiddly at this point).

5 Fold in each corner as shown.

6 Now lift each of the flaps at the back and bend and tuck to create the curvy lotus petal shape.

7 Your finished model will look like this.

8 Using two slightly larger sheets of washi paper, 20cm/8in square, one the same colour and the other in green for the leaves, make two more models. Glue the first model inside the larger model of the same colour, alternating the petals as shown in the photo. Finally, glue the finished flower inside the green model.

5 Amaryllis

★ ★ ★

The gorgeous amaryllis is a bulbous plant with showy, bell-shaped flowers. This model looks best with three or five flowers on a single stem. It works beautifully with single-sided paper, as the white reverse simulates the flower's distinctive patterning.

1 Make a preliminary base and lift the flap, as shown.

2 Open the flap and flatten it down into a kite shape.

3 Turn the model over and repeat steps 1–2 on this side.

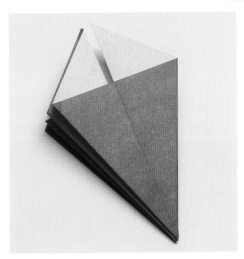

4 Repeat with the remaining two flaps, using the centre fold as your guide.

5 Fold to the centre along the creases, as shown.

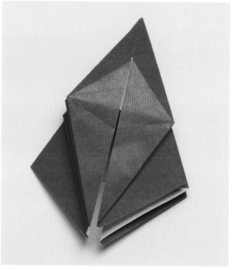
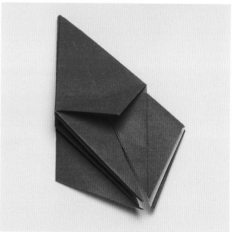

6 Open the flaps you have just made and open the flap beneath, creasing it to make a kite shape.

7 Fold down the small flap. Repeat steps 5–7 on the other three flaps.

8 Ensuring that the model is in the position shown in the photo, fold in both sides to the centre crease.

9 The model will look like this. Repeat step 8 with the remaining three panels.

10 The model should look like this.

11 Fold down each of the four petals, using a pencil to give each one a curl.

12 Make two more flowers and attach each one to a stem made from a pipe cleaner wrapped in florist's tape.

Twist the stems together to make the amaryllis.

INNER PETALS

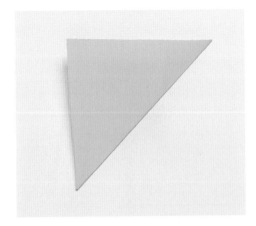

1 Fold your square of paper in half on the diagonal.

2 Fold both corners to the centre.

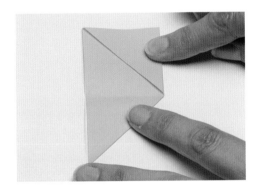

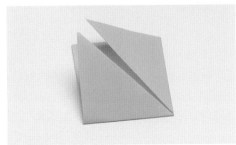

6 Columbine

★

The columbine, aquilegia or 'granny's bonnet' is a cottage-garden favourite. It is a graceful, semi-wild plant that comes in lots of different colours and varieties. I've used a mauve–yellow combination for my model, but you can use more or less any colour you like. Columbines are delicate flowers so you need to use a small size of paper here.

3 Fold the flaps outwards and crease as shown.

4 Flatten down.

  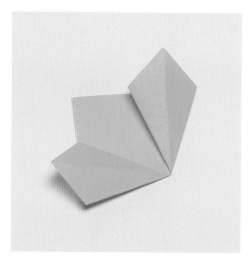

5 Open the pocket and make a squash fold. Do this on both sides. (The crease should be down the centre of each pocket.)

6 Your model should look like this.

 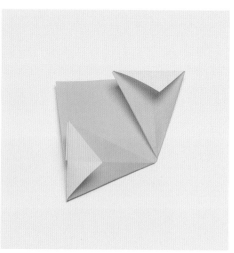 

7 Fold down the tips, as shown.

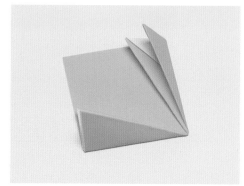

8 Now fold inwards along the centre line.

9 Bring the outer edges together and secure with a little glue. This is the first section of the flower; make four more pieces the same.

OUTER PETALS

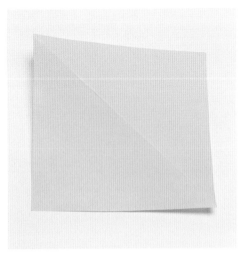

1 Fold your square of paper in half on the diagonal.

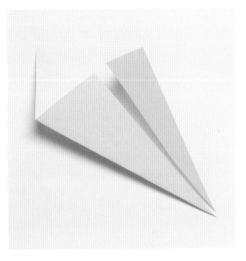

2 Fold the edges to the centre to make a kite shape.

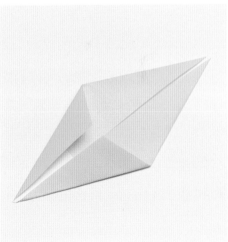

3 Fold in the corners of the kite, as shown.

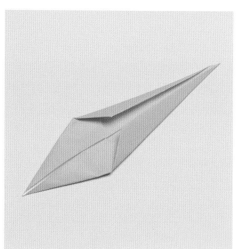

4 Fold in the sides of the kite.

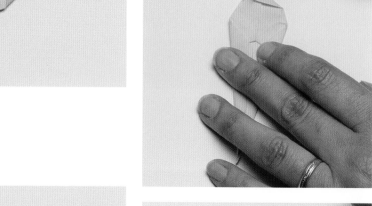

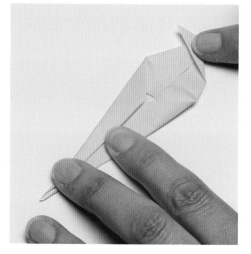

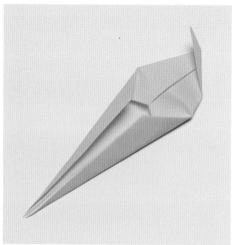

5 Make a diagonal fold at the tip.

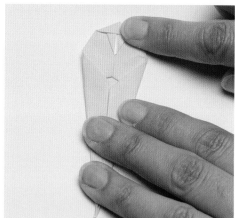

6 Now fold the tip back over in the opposite direction and flatten it.

7 Turn the model over and roll the edges to make them more rounded.

8 Make four more petals like this, and glue the flower together as shown.

9 Attach the flowers to a stem made from pipe cleaners wrapped in florist's tape.

7 Bamboo

★★★

Bamboo is a tall, tree-like member of the grass family, renowned throughout history for its beauty and usefulness. For this model, you will work with rectangular shapes cut down from 15cm (6in) square paper – one large rectangle and several smaller ones – as well as some small squares. You could use double-sided paper in different shades of green, or even patterned paper.

STEM

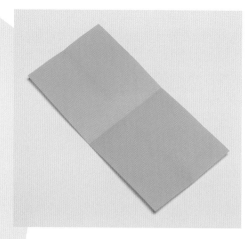

1 Fold the large rectangle in half both ways, and reopen it.

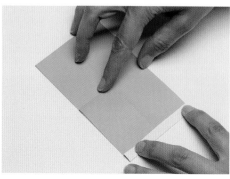

2 Make a pleat fold in the middle of the paper, then fold up the bottom.

3 Turn the paper over and fold down the top corners.

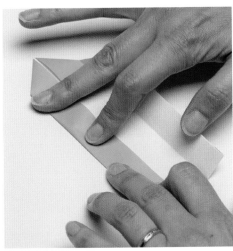

4 Now fold the sides in to the centre.

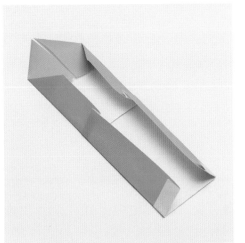

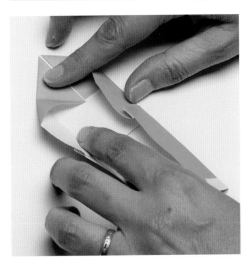

5 Your model should look like this (top). Reopen it on one side.

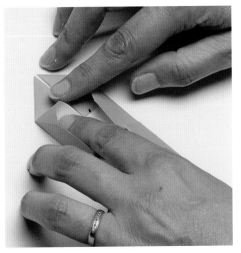

6 Unfold the top of the left-hand flap to make a horizontal crease, then close it. Do the same with the other flap.

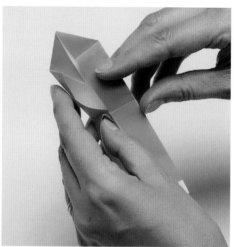

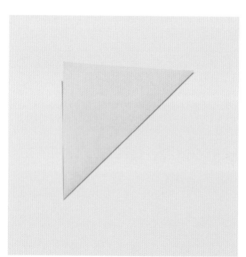

7 The model will look like this.

8 Tuck the right-hand flap inside the left-hand flap to close the shape.

LEAF

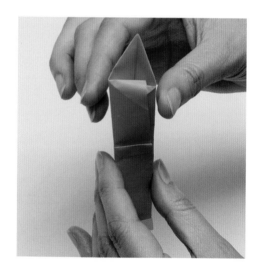

9 Mould the shape gently to make it more rounded. Now make two more the same, using smaller rectangles.

1 Using a small sheet of paper measuring 7.5cm (3in) square, valley fold along the diagonal, as shown.

2 Make a diagonal crease, and fold down so that the edge is in line with the fold.

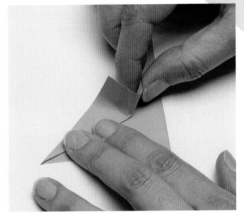

 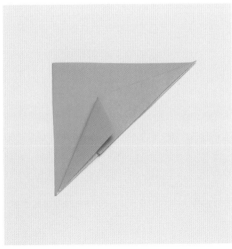

3 Make another diagonal mountain fold.

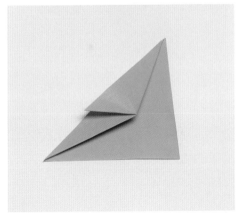

4 Rotate the model 180°, open the flap, and flatten down.

6 Open the flap and press down to make a tiny kite shape.

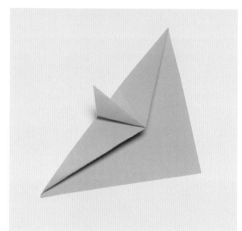

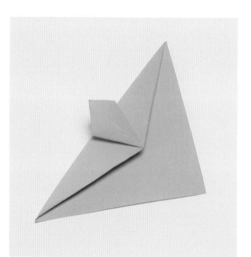

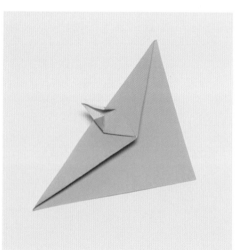

5 Lift the flap in the centre and crease it diagonally. Flatten down.

7 Fold in the tip.

8 Open the flap and flatten it down so that it looks like the second image, above.

 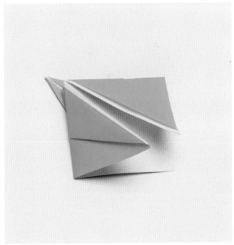

9 Fold the tip down and turn the model over.

10 Fold down the side flaps to meet in the centre.

11 Inside reverse fold the flaps on each side.

12 Fold the model in half along its length.

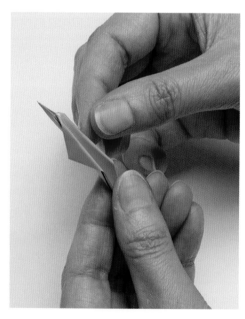

13 Make downward diagonal folds to the top of the model and the tip.

16 Assemble the model by glueing the leaves to the bamboo stems you have made.

14 Now turn the model over and gently pull apart the top flaps.

15 Your final design should look like this. Make another five leaves the same.

8 Calla lily
★

Calla lilies, also known as arum or trumpet lilies, are striking flowers often used in wedding decorations and bridal bouquets. The famous form is white, but they come in a surprising range of colours including pink, green, yellow, purple and orange. I made my final model in white, but have used coloured paper to show the folding process.

FLOWER

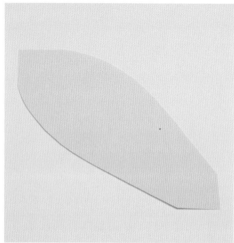

1 Draw the outline of the calla in pencil on a square sheet of paper and cut it out.

2 Turn the paper over and fold up the bottom.

3 Fold in the right-hand side on the diagonal towards the centre. **4** Make the same fold on the left-hand side.

5 Curve in the two long sides and glue the model at the bottom to keep its shape.

FLORAL SPIKE

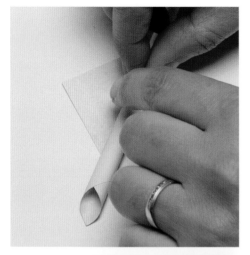

2 Secure it with glue and fix it inside the flower.

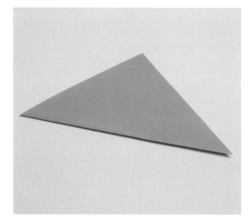

1 Take a small square of paper and roll it up, starting with a corner.

LEAF AND STEM

1 Fold a square of paper on the diagonal and reopen it.

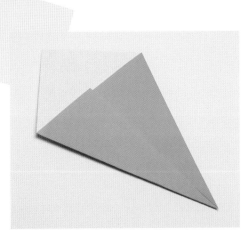

2 Fold both edges to the centre to make a kite shape.

3 Fold the corners to the centre.

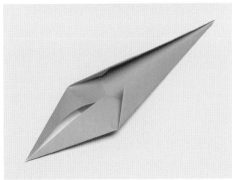

4 Now fold the sides in again to make a narrow shape.

5 For the stem, take a pipe cleaner and glue it to the back of the flower. Wrap florist's tape around the pipe cleaner, starting from the bottom. Fold the leaf in half and attach it to the stem. Mould the tip of the leaf to give a rounded shape.

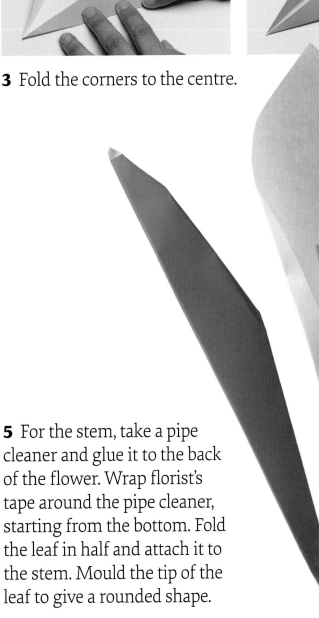

9 Dahlia

★★

Originally from Mexico and Central and South America, dahlias are colourful flowers that come in a number of interesting shapes. The one I have made has petals that spiral around a slightly flattened centre.

FLOWER (OUTER FLORETS)

1 Fold a small square of paper on the diagonal, but off-centre.

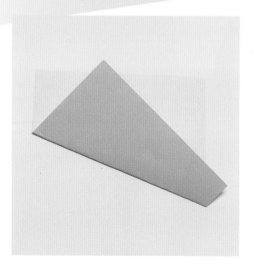  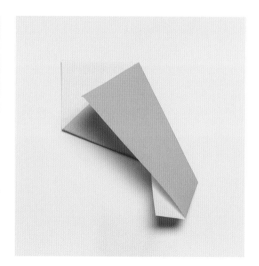

2 Fold the other side in, again on the diagonal.

3 Turn the model over.

4 Fold in from the right, as shown.

5 Turn the model over again and open up the flap.

6 Fold up the lower part on the diagonal, as shown.

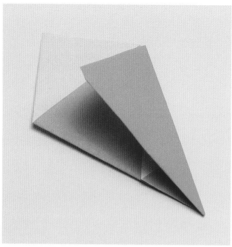

7 Close the shape to give the model above right.

8 Fold down the tip to make a small triangle.

9 Fold up the bottom part as shown.

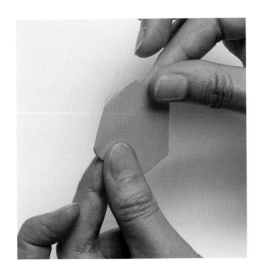

10 Turn the model over. This is your finished petal. You need to make 24 more the same.

11 Start to glue the bases of the petals together, overlapping them in a circle. You need to make three layers to give the spiral shape.

FLOWER (INNER FLORETS)

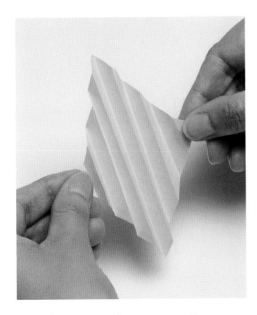

1 Take a small square of paper and create concertina folds.

2 Pinch in the middle and valley fold together. Make three of these.

PUTTING IT ALL TOGETHER

Push the stamens through the centre of the flower and fix with glue. Take a pipe cleaner and glue it to the back of the flower. Wrap the florist's tape around the pipe cleaner, starting from the bottom. Following the instructions for the Calla lily leaf on pages 48–9, make two leaves and attach them to the stem.

10 Campanula
★ ★

There are many different types of campanula. This one, the giant bellflower, has lovely mauvey-blue blooms. It is best made with double-sided paper, perhaps in two different shades of blue (see my final model on page 58).

1 Take a small square of paper and make a preliminary base. Lift and open the flap, as shown.

2 Flatten to make a kite shape. Rotate the model.

4 Rotate the model and open the flap.

3 Fold in the sides to the centre, as shown.

5 Crease and flatten to create a kite shape.

6 Fold up the top flaps from the bottom.

7 Tuck the points up inside the shape.

8 Fold down the small flap.

9 Repeat steps 2–8 on the other side of the model to give this result (above right).

10 Fold up the points so that the finished flower looks like a pixie hat. Mould the shape to make it more rounded.

PUTTING IT ALL TOGETHER
Make at least seven flowers. Now take one long pipe cleaner and seven short pieces and wrap them all in florist's tape. Insert the short pipe cleaner pieces into the flowers and twist the ends to secure them. Attach the flowers to the long pipe cleaner to make the campanula stem.

FLOWER

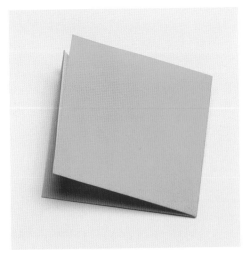

1 Start with a square of paper folded into a preliminary base.

11 Camellia

⭐ ⭐ ⭐

The 'rose of winter', camellias provide an exotic splash of colour when little else is in flower. I have used a twisting technique to create the characteristic shape. You could use single-sided paper for this model, but double-sided works best.

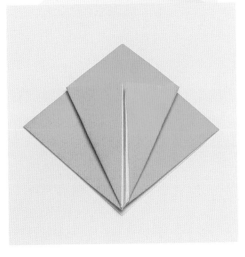

2 With the open end at the bottom, fold the sides to the centre to make a kite shape.

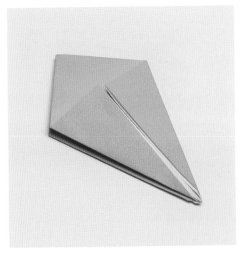

3 Turn the model over and repeat step 2 on the other side.

4 Fold down the top as shown.

5 Unfold, and open the flaps. Press down along the creases you have created to make a diamond shape.

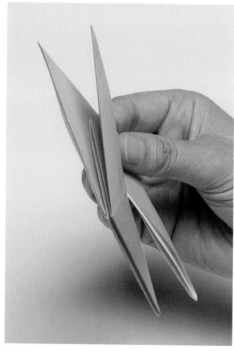

7 This folding gives you a bird base, shown left.

6 Turn the model over and repeat steps 4–5 on the other side.

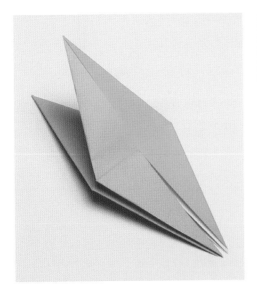

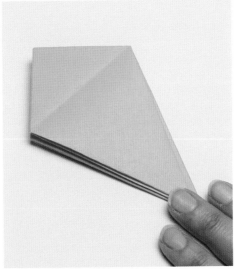

8 Starting with your bird base points at the bottom, fold down the flaps on both sides. Rotate the model.

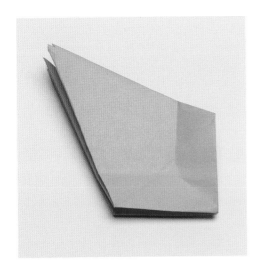

9 Make a valley fold down the middle and open out again. Now crease diagonally on both sides, ensuring that the crease is made parallel to the edge.

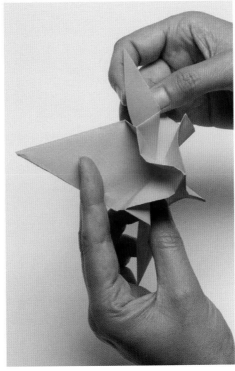

10 Start to open the model gently, pulling and twisting the four flaps until they are roughly equidistant from one another. Keep hold of the base as you do this.

11 Turn the model over and keep twisting. You can see the flower starting to take shape.

14 Turn the model over.

12 On a flat surface, arrange the model into the camellia shape, then turn it over.

13 Fold each of the points to the centre.

15 With a pair of tweezers, twist the flower to make a tighter centre.

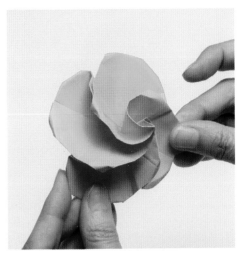

16 Roll the edges of the petals to give a more rounded shape.

LEAF

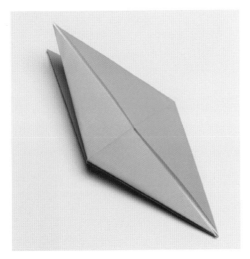

1 Repeat steps 1–7 of the camellia flower to create another bird base.

2 Fold down both flaps.

3 Make diagonal folds as shown. Repeat on the other side.

4 Make a fold so that you can hold the model while opening it.

PUTTING IT ALL TOGETHER

Open out and curl the leaves with a pencil. Then make another leaf model. Glue the flower in the middle of the leaf arrangement. Wrap a pipe cleaner in florist's tape and attach it to the back of the leaves.

12 **Daffodil**

★ ★ ★

The daffodil belongs to the narcissus genus of plants, spring flowering bulbs that are generally yellow or white in colour, sometimes with a contrasting central cup. Many types of Narcissus *have a powerful fragrance. With their unmistakable shape and colour, daffodils are hugely popular as ornamental flowers and have been celebrated in art and literature. The daffodil is the national flower of Wales and the chosen symbol of cancer charities in many countries. It is also a symbol of new beginning.*

OUTER PETALS
15 X 15 CM PAPER

This piece is created using a hexagonal base.

1 Fold the paper in half along the diagonal.

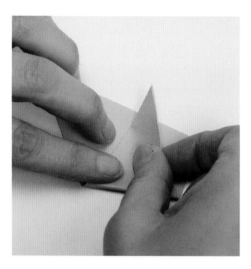  

2 Fold in the left-hand point along the dotted lines, as shown. Be sure that your folds are equidistant from the top of the triangle.

 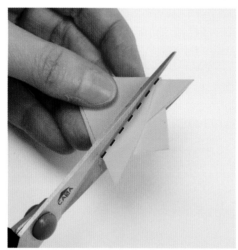 

3 Fold over the right-hand point on top.

4 Cut along the dotted line and open out the model.

5 This is your hexagonal base.

6 Fold the model until you have 12 equal sections, as shown.

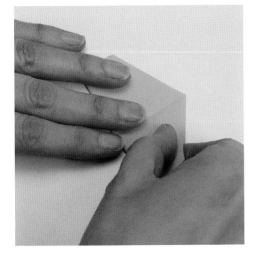

7 Pinch the centre point and push in the sides, folding until you have the shape

8 This is what the model looks like from above.

9 Fold the sides towards the centre and flatten down.

10 Work your way round the model, folding in all the other flaps.

11 Fold up the tip.

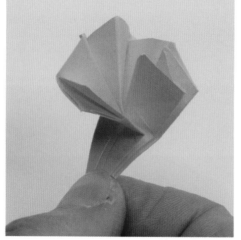

12 Your model should look like this.

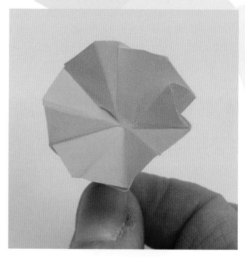

13 Holding the part just folded, open the petals from the top slowly.

INNER PETALS
15 X 15 CM PAPER

Repeat steps 1–10 for the outer petals.

1 Repeat the folding along the vertical lines, as shown. Make these folds on all the sides.

2 Slowly open just the very top to make the internal petals.

3 Tuck the long tube into the centre of the outer petals, then make a small hole in the base for attaching it to the stem.

STEM WITH LEAF
18 X 18 CM PAPER

1 Valley fold along on the diagonal. Then fold in the sides along the dotted lines to make a kite shape.

2 Fold along the dotted lines as shown. This gives a diamond shaped model.

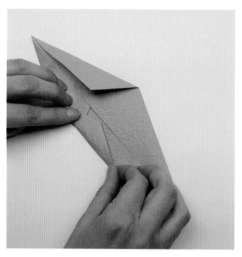

3 Fold the sides towards the centre along the dotted lines.

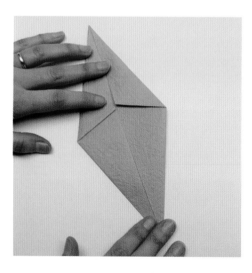

4 Fold in again along the dotted lines as shown, so that the sides meet in the middle.

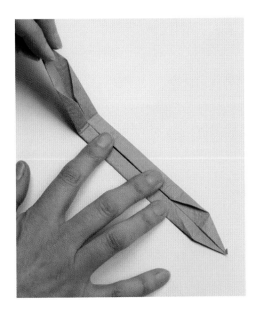  

5 Fold the left-hand tip across along the dotted line. Close the model and rotate so that the left-hand side forms the base.

6 Fold the left-hand tip across along the dotted line. Close the model and rotate so that the left-hand side forms the base.

7 Your model is now ready for you to add the flower.

1 Valley fold in half along the diagonal.

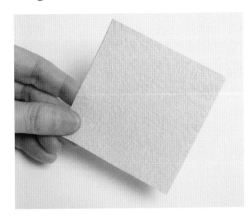

13 Passion flower

★ ★

Passion flowers are vines native to the Americas. This one has striking white and purple-blue flowers with five greenish-yellow stamens. The fruit is a type of berry; it can be yellow or dark purple and it has a juicy interior filled with seeds. In traditional medicine it has been used as a sedative, and is believed to relieve a range of ailments, including anxiety and insomnia.

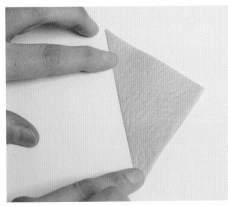

2 Reopen the model.

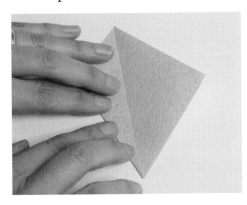

PETALS
7 X 5CM (10 SHEETS)

3 Fold along the dotted lines to make a kite shape.

4 Fold again along the dotted lines.

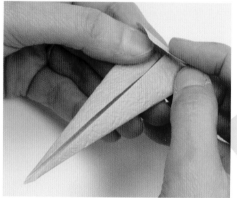

5 Fold the top triangle on the left over the top of the shape.

6 Fold in the corners, as shown.

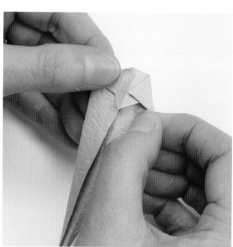

7 Fold in the point on the right.

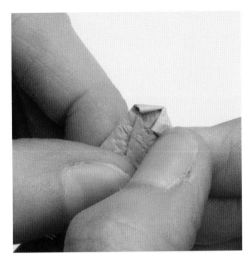

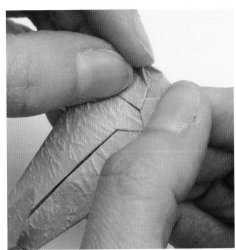

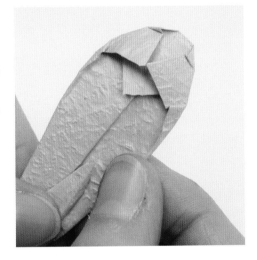

8 Model the piece to give a rounded shape, and turn it over.

Repeat for the remaining nine petals.

CENTRE
5 X 5CM PAPER (4 SHEETS)

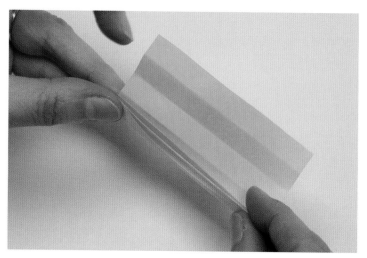 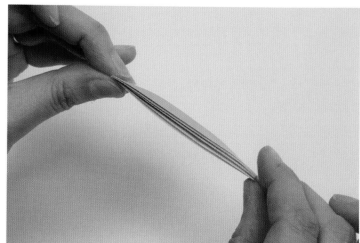

1 Accordion-fold the paper.

2 Fold it in half and glue the inner sides.

3 Make another three pieces.
4 Glue the outer sides together.

STAMENS
4 X 4CM PAPER (5 SHEETS)

1 Valley fold in half along the horizontal.

2 Reopen the model. **3** Valley fold the sides in to the centre line.

4 Repeat

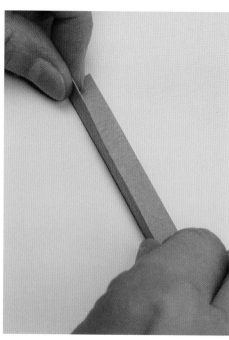

5 Close the shape and rotate it 45 degrees.

6 Fold down the top along the dotted line, as shown.

7 Open it up again.

 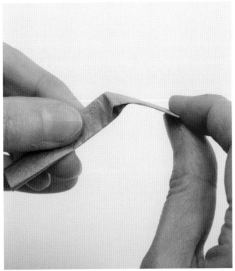 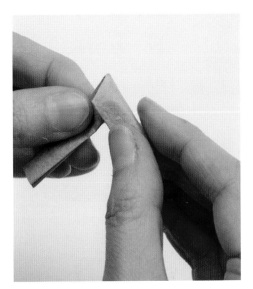

8 Push down opened up top part while keeping lower part folded.

9 Push back top part to create a bevelled fold.

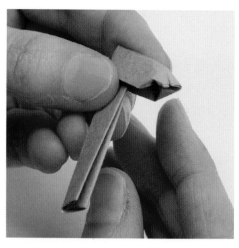

10 Shape the model to make it rounder.

Use a dab of glue to attach the petals behind the centre of the flower. Then add the stamens to the top of the flower centre.